WORD PROBLEM$
WITH MONEY

PORTIA SUMMERS

Enslow Publishing
101 W. 23rd Street
Suite 240
New York, NY 10011
USA

enslow.com

WORDS TO KNOW

add–To count and make a total number.

bill–Paper money.

change–Money returned to as the balance of the amount paid.

currency–The kind of money a country uses.

dollar–The American currency.

subtract–To take away.

value–The worth of something.

CONTENTS

A QUICK LOOK AT MONEY

penny	nickel	dime	quarter	half-dollar	one-dollar coin
1¢	5¢	10¢	25¢	50¢	$1

one-dollar bill
$1

five-dollar bill
$5

ten-dollar bill
$10

twenty-dollar bill
$20

WORD PROBLEMS WITH MONEY

You can solve word problems about money using four steps:

1) Read the problem.

Irina has 3 dimes and 4 pennies. How much money does Irina have?

2) Plan how to solve the problem.
What does the problem ask you to figure out? How many cents Irina has.
How can you find the answer? Count the value of the coins Irina has.

3) Follow the plan.
Count the value of the coins, starting with the most valuable (the dimes). For dimes, count by tens, and for the pennies count by ones.
Irina has 34¢.

4) Check your work.
Did you count the right coins?
Count the coins again. Is the answer the same?

10¢   20¢   30¢   31¢   32¢   33¢   34¢

Luis had 50¢. He found a quarter. How much money does Luis have in all?

Plan how to solve the problem. What does it ask you to find? *How much money Luis has in all.* How can you find the answer? *Add the amount Luis found to the amount he started with.*

Follow the plan. How much money did Luis start with? 50¢.

How much did Luis find? *A quarter.*

What's the value of a quarter? 25¢.

50¢ + 25¢ = 75¢

Check your work.

Luis started with 50¢.

Luis found a quarter, which equals 25¢.

50¢ + 25¢ = 75¢

HOW MUCH IS LEFT?

Read the problem.
Will had $8. He used $5 to pay for his lunch. How many dollars does Will have left?

Plan how to solve it.
What does the problem ask you to find? *How many dollars Will has left.*

How can you find the answer? Subtract *the amount Will spent from the amount he started with.*

Follow the plan.
Will started with $8. He spent $5.
  $8 – $5 = $3
Will has $3 left.

Check your work.

Did you start with the right amount? Did you subtract the right amount?
Check your math.

$8 - $5 = $3

WHO HAS MORE?

Read the problem.
Genera has 3 dimes and 4 pennies. Bianca has 1 quarter and 3 nickels. Who has more money?

Plan how to solve the problem.
What does the problem ask you to find? *Who has more money.*

How can you find the answer? *Count how much money each girl has. Then compare to see who has more.*

Follow the plan.
How much money does Genera have? She has 3 dimes and 4 pennies.
Count the value of 3 dimes and 4 pennies.
10¢   20¢   30¢   31¢   32¢   33¢   34¢

How much money does Bianca have? She has 1 quarter and 3 nickels.
Count the value of 1 quarter and 3 nickels.
25¢   30¢   35¢   40¢

Which is more?
40¢ is more than 34¢. Bianca has more money than Genera.

Check your work.
Count the value of each girl's coins again. Did you count the same amounts?

IS IT ENOUGH?

Read the problem.
Ahmed has 3 dimes and 12 pennies. A marker costs 39¢.
Does he have enough money to buy it?

Plan how to solve the problem.
What does the problem ask you to find?
If Ahmed has enough money to buy a marker.
How can you find the answer? *Find the value of 3 dimes and 12 pennies by adding the value of the dimes and pennies. Compare this amount to the price of a marker.*

Follow the plan.
How much is 3 dimes and 12 pennies worth?
3 dimes = 30¢.
12 pennies = 12¢.
30¢ + 12¢ = 42¢
42¢ is more than 39¢.

Ahmed has enough money to buy a marker.

Check your work.
Did you answer the right question?
Count the coins again. Did you get the same answer?

Read the problem.
Camilla has a ten-dollar bill. A poster costs $5. A notebook costs $6. Does she have enough to buy both?

Plan how to solve the problem.
What does the problem ask? *If Camilla has enough for a poster and a notebook together.* How can you find the answer? *Add the cost of the poster and the notebook and compare it to the amount that Camilla has to find out if she has enough.*

There are three mints in the United States. All of the money used in the United States is printed or stamped in Denver, Colorado; San Francisco, California; or Philadelphia, Pennsylvania. The mint in Philadelphia is the largest in the world.

Follow the plan.
Add the cost of the poster ($5) and the cost of the notebook ($6).

$5 + $6 = $11
poster   notebook

Camilla has a ten-dollar bill. A ten-dollar bill is worth $10.
The poster and the notebook together cost $11.
$10 is less than $11.
Camilla does not have enough to buy a poster and a notebook.

Check your work.
Did you add correctly?

HOW MUCH CHANGE?

Read the problem.

A piece of candy costs 35¢. Daphne paid for it with 2 quarters. How much change will Daphne get back?

Plan how to solve the problem.

What does the problem ask you to find? *How much change Daphne will get.*

How can you find the answer? *Start with the amount Daphne used to pay for the candy. Subtract the price of the candy.*

Follow the plan.
Daphne paid for the candy
 with 2 quarters.
2 quarters = 50¢.

50¢ – 35¢ = 15¢
Daphne will get 15¢.

Check your work.
Add the amount of the change to the cost of the candy.
15¢ + 35¢ = 50¢

CHANGE FROM A DOLLAR

Read the problem.

Maurizio bought lemonade at a stand for 64¢. He paid with a one-dollar bill. He was given the least number of coins possible in change. What coins did Maurizio get?

Plan to solve the problem.

What does the problem ask you to find? *The coins Maurizio got as change.* How can you find the answer? *Subtract to find the amount of change and decide what coins were used to make the change.*

Follow the plan.

Maurizio paid with a one-dollar bill, worth $1, or 100¢. He spent 64¢.

100¢ – 64¢ = 36¢

Maurizio's change was 36¢.

Make 36¢ using as many of the most valuable coins as you can without going over.

One quarter is worth 25¢. One dime more makes 35¢. One penny more is 36¢.

Check your work.
Count the value of the coins you used. Do they equal 36¢?

Read the problem.

You sold a candy bar for 79¢. You were paid with a one-dollar bill. You gave 21¢ in change.

How can you make sure the change is correct?

Plan how to solve the problem.

What does the problem ask? *How you can count back change.* How do you count back change? *Start with the amount something costs, then count on. When the change is all counted, the total should be the amount paid.*

Practice counting and making change on your own.

LEARN MORE

BOOKS

American Education Publishing. *The Complete Book of Time and Money, Grades K-3*. Greensboro, NC: 2009.

Furgang, Kathy. *Kids Everything Money: A Wealth of Facts, Photos, and Fun*. Washington, DC: National Geographic Children's Books, 2013.

WEBSITES

H.I.P. Pocket Change

www.usmint.gov/kids

The official website of the United States Mint

Science Kids

www.sciencekids.co.nz/sciencefacts/technology/ money.html

Learn fun facts about money!

INDEX

Published in 2017 by Enslow Publishing, LLC.
101 W. 23rd Street, Suite 240, New York, NY 10011

Copyright © 2017 by Enslow Publishing, LLC.
All rights reserved.

No part of this book may be reproduced by any means without the written permission of the publisher.

Library of Congress Cataloging-in-Publication Data
Names: Summers, Portia, author.
Title: Word problems with money / Portia Summers.
Description: New York, NY : Enslow Publishing, [2017] | Series: The value of money | Includes bibliographical references and index.
Identifiers: LCCN 2015046325| ISBN 9780766077133 (library bound) | ISBN 9780766077072 (pbk.) | ISBN 9780766077102 (6-pack)
Subjects: LCSH: Money--United States--Juvenile literature. | Word problems (Mathematics)--Juvenile literature.
Classification: LCC HG221.5 .S863 2016 | DDC 332.4/040973--dc23
LC record available at http://lccn.loc.gov/2015046325

Printed in Malaysia

To Our Readers: We have done our best to make sure all website addresses in this book were active and appropriate when we went to press. However, the author and the publisher have no control over and assume no liability for the material available on those websites or on any websites they may link to. Any comments or suggestions can be sent by e-mail to customerservice@enslow.com.

Portions of this book originally appeared in the book *I Can Do Money Word Problems* by Rebecca Wingard-Nelson.

Photo Credits: Cover (green dollar sign background, used throughout the book) Rachael Arnott/Shutterstock.com, Fedorov Oleksiy/Shutterstock.com; (white dollar sign background, used throughout the book) Golden Shrimp/Shutterstock.com; VIGE.COM/Shutterstock.com (piggy bank with dollar sign, used throughout book); Golden Shrimp/Shutterstock.com (green cross pattern border, used throughout book); p. 2 skodonnell/iStockphoto.com; p. 3 STILLFX/Shutterstock.com; p.4 penny (used throughout the book), mattesimages/Shutterstock.com; nickel (used throughout the book), United States Mint image; dime and quarter (used throughout the book), B Brown/Shutterstock.com; half-dollar, Daniel D Malone/Shutterstock.com; one-dollar coin, JordiDelgado/iStockphoto.com; one-dollar, five-dollar and twenty-dollar bills (used throughout the book) Anton_Ivanov/Shutterstock.com; ten-dollar bill, Pavel Kirichenko/Shutterstock.com; p. 5, 11 JGI/Jamie Grill/Blend Images/Getty Images; p. 8 Andersen Ross/Iconica/Getty Images; p. 9 vinnstock/Shutterstock.com; p. 11 Polka Dot Images/Thinkstock.com; p. 13 David Sacks/Digital Vision/Thinkstock; p. 15 Joseph Sohm/Shutterstock.com; p. 16 zig4photo/iStockphoto.com; p. 17 Glow Images/Getty Images; p. 18 Glenn Asakawa/Denver Post/Getty Images; p. 20 Christopher Robbins/Digital Vision/Thinkstock; P. 21 Jamie Grill/Tetra Images/Getty Images.